MW00323471

High Achiever:
Advice to New High-School Teachers

Dory Smith

Parson's Porch Books

High Achiever: Advice to New High-School Teachers

ISBN: Softcover 978-1-951472-73-3

Copyright © 2020 by Dory Smith

The author's photo on the back cover was provided by **Mike Carlson Photography.**

All rights reserved. No part of this book may be reproduced or transmitted in any form or by any means, electronic or mechanical, including photocopying, recording, or by any information storage and retrieval system, without permission in writing from the publisher.

www.parsonsporch.com

High Achiever:
Advice to New High-School
Teachers

Contents

Introduction

I retired from teaching this year (2020) after thirty years in high school. When I started teaching, we still typed everything on electric typewriters and then had someone in the office run copies on a mimeograph machine. (I can still smell that warm ink!) The coolest technology I used was a reel-to-reel movie projector and a filmstrip projector that advanced by itself instead of giving me the beep to advance it.

From that first year in 1989, I saw the projector morph briefly into a giant laser video disc (the size of a record album), and then into the DVDs that I air-played onto my Apple TV. At one time I had purchased my own LCD projector since we had only a few in the whole school for teachers to check out. Now, it sits on a shelf because nobody wants it.

I spent a lot of time in the early nineties confiscating pagers, since only doctors and drug dealers needed to carry them. Later I told kids that they were crazy if they thought I could not see the glow of their forbidden cell phones in the dark half hour before school started. However, in the last few years I kept an iPad in my classroom for kids to use during class when they did not have a phone of their own.

I have always dreaded having to call parents – as probably most teachers do. When I started, I had to go to the clinic or office to get parents' phone numbers and then to a workroom to find a phone. Eventually we got phones in our classroom, and one of my favorite discipline techniques was to look up the parent's phone number on my electronic gradebook and call them from my classroom during class: "I just thought you'd like to know what your son is doing in my class right now. Oh, of course you can talk to him!" Covid-19 and distance learning raised my game even higher, though, when I got my Google Voice number and could then text parents from home. I really wish I had had that sooner!

Although much has changed over thirty years, the fundamentals have not. I am still friends with Cyndee Smith, who supervised my internship and then was my first department head, and the skills and concepts she taught me then are the same skills and concepts that I have honed and taught to my own interns and to the first-year teachers I have mentored. Thank you, Cyndee, for your patience as I learned these lessons.

For you, Reader, I have tried to write this guide the way I would want to read it. Do not feel the need to read it from beginning to end. Instead, go to the chapter that you need now, and then read the rest when you have time. Trust me, I know how stretched your time is: and I promise not to waste it. Keep in mind that I spent my career in high school, and while this information will work for middle school as well, I cannot speak with any authority on teaching elementary students. You folks are on your own!

Chapter One

Grading

Grading was the bane of my existence. As an English teacher, I am positive that we grade more than any other discipline. In fact, I caught the flu every year, and I am convinced that the reason I got sick so often is that I touched so many infected papers. That said, here are the most important things I learned about grading:

Answer it yourself first.

Take the test; do the worksheet; answer the questions. Do not just depend on the answer key provided by the publisher. If you get confused by a question, so will your students. If you created the assignment yourself, answering it yourself will also reveal any embarrassing typos.

Too many times as a young teacher, I relied on the answer key that came with the assignment. Of course, I had read through the assignment before I gave it to them, but when I went over the assignment with my students, they sometimes would ask me why the answer was right. When I could not answer well, I really hated looking unprepared in front of my class.

Be consistent.

Sometimes I envy math teachers; right is right and wrong is wrong. English and history teachers do not always have that luxury. We spend a lot of time deciding whether this kid really has an idea of what the answer is and just cannot put it into the right words or whether he is completely off base.

Do not spend forever deciding how much partial credit to assign. Decide and then WRITE IT DOWN, preferably on the answer key you just created. I kept these annotated answer keys in my file cabinet, and in the last few years I scanned them into my computer.

You do not have to grade everything, but you do have to grade when they do not expect you to.

The first year I taught honors English, my students came in with a summer assignment that I myself would have struggled with. It was long and complicated and full of essay responses. As I graded, I noticed some brilliant work, but I stopped being impressed when I saw the same exact brilliance written verbatim in a few more papers. When I dealt with the plagiarism the next day, a student confided in me that since the summer work was so complicated, they had decided as a group that I would probably not grade it. That was a big lesson for me. If students require weeks to complete an assignment, they deserve for me to spend the time it takes to grade it well.

When you have 150 students, they must know that you will grade their work, or they just will not do it! My students loved to tell me about the stupid answers they turned in when they knew their other teachers were grading only for completion and not for accuracy. However, you can get really bogged down trying to grade every answer of a twenty-two-question worksheet on *Romeo and Juliet* Act I from 150 students.

So, here is what I did: grade the first few papers, at least five or ten, just to get a feel for the students' answers (after you have already created your key). Make sure you select papers from different class periods if you have allowed students to work together. When you do this, you will see that some answers are gimmes— everyone gets them right. Some, however, are much harder. Those are the only questions you will grade for accuracy.

On your answer key, star or highlight the questions you have selected. Then as you grade each paper, check to make sure every question has an answer. Mark the blank answers wrong. Then grade the accuracy questions. Do not write the right answers in for them; just mark them right or wrong. When you return the papers, you should go over the answers with your class and have students write the correct answers on their own papers. After all, (I would remind them) this will probably be their study guide for the test.

At times, I have had five classes of freshmen, all handing in the same review assignment on *Romeo and Juliet* Act III. That comes out to about 150 copies of the same double-sided short-answer assignment! After

I graded the first few papers, I noticed that there were just three or four answers that students tended to miss (since it was a review assignment, the rest were easy to find in the text). Then it was easy. I scanned each paper, marked blank answers incorrect, and then scrutinized only those four. Since the assignment had twenty-five questions total, everyone who completed it got at least twenty-one correct out of twenty-five (an 84%), and I finished grading in one hour instead of several.

You are asking yourself right now (or you should be) what happens when a student notices a wrong answer that you did not mark wrong because it was not on your list. DO NOT say that you do not grade every answer. You could use the tried and true "Oops, how did I miss that?" However, a better option is—before you give them the right answers—to say that you graded some questions leniently, but you want them to have the best answers to study before the test. As I called out answers, I often would ask whether anyone had a different answer from mine that they wanted to ask about. This led to discussions of why certain answers were better than others and did not let on to students that I did not grade the whole assignment.

Finally, when they ask, "Is this for a grade?" you answer, "Everything is for a grade!"

Trade and Grade

Having students trade papers and grade each other's work is controversial. Many school systems do not even allow the practice because of student privacy. However, I have found this to be one of my favorite teaching tools.

The first time each year that I had students trade and grade, I told them that this was voluntary. If they preferred not to allow someone else to grade their paper, they could give it to me to grade. However, if they asked me to grade it for them, they probably would not get it back as quickly.

I would have them trade (or even trade twice). You can tell them to pass it to the person behind them (and then pass it again) and then have the person at the back bring her paper up to the front.

"Now take out something to grade with that is different from what is used on the paper. If the paper is in pencil, take out a pen. If the paper is in ink, take out a different color." I usually would have colored pens or even highlighters for students to borrow.

"Write your name at the bottom of the paper you're grading." During this time, I wandered the aisle to see that students were complying. Then I called out the answers, glancing at student papers to make sure they were grading correctly. If the answers were potentially confusing, I would have made a PowerPoint slide with

15

the answers and used a presentation remote to reveal only one answer at a time while I continued around the classroom.

The reason I like this method so much is not just because it saved me time grading (and I really do like that part!). The real reason is that while I called out the answers, I also EXPLAINED. Grading time was teaching time for me. I used this method most with vocabulary worksheets so I could give examples and explain nuances as I called out the answers. Some teachers would tell you to grade the papers yourself and then explain the answers when you return them. If your school says you must do this, then do it. However, students are far less likely to listen to your explanation when they already have a grade at the top of the paper. They want to know only why they got these wrong (and many do not even care about that!) and do not care about the explanations for the ones they got right.

At the beginning of the year, I would take up the papers to record the scores, holding the students accountable for their grading. After a few weeks, when they knew me better (and vice versa) I would call names and have them tell me their scores.

Plagiarism and Cheating

Especially if you teach English, plagiarism is a multi-faceted problem. Before you deal with your students, you need to clarify several issues for yourself.

As a teacher of freshmen, I knew that part of my job was to teach students how not to cheat. Middle school had taught them to use sources in their writing; my job was to teach them how to use these sources appropriately, and I told my kids this up front. You cannot tell kids not to cheat or not to plagiarize without defining those terms well.

These are not first-day-of-school lessons. These are lessons you must teach as you encounter them. Therefore, the first time I assigned group work, I told them explicitly that they may not "divide and conquer." Say to your students: The purpose of assigning you to do this in a group is that you work together on each question and that you discuss and learn from each other. Dividing the work just gets it done faster, but you do not learn from it.

Similarly, when I assigned a piece that required sources, I spent a lot of time teaching them how to cite those sources. I gave examples of correct and incorrect use of sources. This may seem time consuming, and it is, but you do not have to do it for every assignment. Teach it well the first time, and then remind them of it afterward.

17

The next issue is to decide for yourself is what to do when you do catch them cheating. The rule I made for myself was to imagine defending my decision to their parents. Go through the possible consequences and decide which one you can most comfortably support. You have several options:

• Give a zero on the assignment with no chance to recover it.

• Allow the student to resubmit the assignment for half credit. Sometimes I also added that they had to redo it in my room during their lunch or after school, explaining that if they had cheated once, then they were likely to do it again.

• Take away points for just the part they cheated on. Be careful with this! I used this option for research papers or other major assignments when giving a zero would devastate a student's grade. I did not use this option on homework or small assignments. Kids are great lawyers and negotiating with them just makes life too hard. If they obviously copied on a small assignment, the whole thing is a zero. This lesson does not cost them much, and it deters them from doing it again later.

• If you discover a group cheating, you can always divide the grade. 100% divided by three group members is a miserable grade, but not a zero.

In all these cases, do not forget to call the parent. Parents want to know about issues of character even more than grades. One thing that makes this phone call more pleasant, though, is to remind the parent that you know they raised their child not to do this, but that students will try anything. I tried to reinforce the idea that the parents and I were on the same team. Remember also not to discuss other students. If parents ask you who else was involved in the cheating, you tell them that you are legally not allowed to talk to them about anyone other than their own child.

Another issue for you to consider is whether what you see is plagiarism. You may see a phrase show up in several papers, or if you use an online plagiarism checker, you may see a similarity highlighted on multiple papers. Sometimes this is totally innocent. The similar phrase may be a line from the prompt that students have included in their answer (as they should), or it may simply be the best or most natural way to say something. Do not let your detection tool do your thinking. Its job is to notice similarities, but you are the teacher and must decide whether the similarity is plagiarism or not. When you make your decision, write it down so you can be consistent.

We will not talk much here about detection tools since new ones come out regularly. I was blessed that my school paid the subscription price for *Turnitin*, but before that we used a lot of Google. When you see that brilliant phrase from a fourteen-year-old, your first emotion is celebration. Then the cynic in you makes you check online to see which genius your little thief stole it from. Learn the difference between a teenager's voice in writing and a published author's voice.

Keep in mind that the kids in your honors classes may indeed be gifted geniuses, but the other side of that coin is that gifted geniuses are often afraid to fail. Honors kids cheat far more than kids in regular classes because they care more about their grades, and they cheat creatively. Go online and search for ways to cheat—you will find more than you ever considered. Educate yourself on these techniques, but the best thing you can do to prevent cheating is to be vigilant. Get the reputation of being the teacher who always catches cheaters. Sometimes you will be wrong. You will think a student is cheating when he is not. Admit it and apologize, but do not let your fear of being wrong cause you to become complacent. When you ask a student about possible cheating, avoid asking yes/no questions. "Did you copy this?" will always be answered by "No." Instead ask, "Why did you copy this?" or "Did the other student give you permission to copy his work?" This is an easier way to get to the truth.

Other than noticing similarities or too-well-turned phrases in written work, the best way I know to catch cheaters is body language. Watch your students take a test. Who looks different? Cheaters look down at their laps. They keep one hand on the desk to write with and the other under the desktop. They wear hoods or caps. They sit crooked. When you see any of these behaviors, quietly walk over to the student and ask her to stand up. You do not have to accuse her of anything, but you will catch her so off guard that the cheat sheet will fall to the floor, or you'll see that her odd movement was something totally innocent. If you catch her cheating, do not make a fuss. Quietly take her paper and whisper that you will talk about it after class. The other students will see, and any other cheating will stop. On the other hand, if you were wrong, just smile and say, "Sorry, I thought I saw something" and walk away—and any other cheating will stop!

A more difficult circumstance of cheating to catch is when multiple classes have done the same assignment, as with summer work. In our school, the English department would assign a reading assignment to all freshmen, for instance. Before we used *Turnitin*, the freshman teachers had to get together as a team and compare notes. It was tedious, but we did catch some. You will have to work with your team to catch this kind of cheating.

Finally, protect your answer keys. Many teachers write the word *KEY* at the top of a paper and leave it on their desk. Why not lay a $20 on top of it and hope nobody takes it? My intern supervisor taught me to

21

write a fake name on the top of my keys, so they do not look like keys. Later, when I started scanning my keys into my computer, I learned to password-protect them. Do not think that students will not break into your computer to get your keys. A few years back, we had a big scandal when an AP kid broke into the AP teacher's computer and posted all his tests and keys online for everyone to see. The higher the level of student, the more likely he is to cheat. If you do not know how to password protect your documents, Google it!

Late Work

Late work will cause you more stress than a bin full of research papers, so set a policy and stick to it. Those teachers who accept late work (even for only partial credit) all the way up to the end of the quarter find themselves working far too hard to get everything done before grades are due. Since I always considered part of my job to teach life skills as well as English, allowing open-ended deadlines seemed counterproductive to me.

However, everyone drops the ball sometimes, and I have always been grateful when someone gave me a break. To that end, I set up some back-up plans that other freshman teachers also emulated, and I wrote them into my syllabus.

1. If you are absent on the day I assign something, you must ask for the assignment on the day you return. It is then due two days later (this was our district policy).
2. If you are present on the day I assign something, but absent the day it is due, then it is due on the day you return—you do not get extra time. (This may seem obvious, but students try to lawyer the district policy into gaining extra time, so I make it clear on the syllabus.)
3. If you do not have your assignment on the due date, you may make it up THAT DAY ONLY during lunch or after school in my classroom. (Since we so often trade and grade in class, they would too easily copy if I allowed them to make it up outside my room.) If you are unable to take advantage of this second chance, the assignment will earn the grade of zero.
4. Large assignments like research papers are too large to make up at lunch. Therefore, you may turn them in late for a 10% grade reduction for each day late, up to 50% off. After five days, the assignment will earn the grade of zero.

Of course, you may have to be flexible on these options. If you have a lunchtime meeting that day, you may make other arrangements with your students, but those flexible arrangements will be the exception, not the rule. I have also had to create a separate policy for my last class, since they clearly could not come in during lunch that day. They could come in before school or during lunch the next day. The point you are making to your students is that you recognize the need for second chances, but they need to manage their time well enough to meet your deadlines.

Another situation for you to consider is extended absences. If a student is out for a week because of the flu or to be in the hospital, you will, of course, give more than two days per absence for make-up work. After all, this student has six classes to make up, not just yours, and if she has been out sick that many days, she probably is not back up to 100% yet. Be gracious in the amount of time you give for make-up work.

Chapter Two

Classroom Management

When I ended my first year of teaching, I nearly failed the beginning teacher program for one reason: poor classroom management. Back then, behavioral systems were the rage. Giving students rewards for good behavior and consequences for bad required hours of work that this first-year teacher just did not have to spare. I had a green page that I had students sign when I "caught" them doing something good and a red page that I wrote their names on when they broke the rules. When they showed up a certain number of times on either page, they earned either a reward or a consequence. It was tedious, and it really did not work.

Over the years, I learned from other teachers what does work, and by the end of my career other teachers were calling on me to teach them how to manage their classrooms.

Set the tone on the first day.

The aphorism when I started teaching was "Don't smile until Christmas." The idea is that you need to start the year sternly and then warm up after you have established your authority. Many excellent teachers deride this adage, but it has some merit. You do not need to be a total jerk, but you do need to set the right tone from the very first day of school.

When my students walked in on the first day of school each year, they saw these instructions on the board (or later the TV screen): "Welcome to English. Look at the seating chart on the podium and find your seat." So, while I was at my door directing lost students to their classes, the kids in my room were already helping each other to follow my directions. Many schedule changes occur the first day of school, so somebody would not find his name on the chart, but I had already planned for that happenstance and had set aside a few empty desks. When the bell rang to start class, I announced that they had just had their first test and that we would now see how well they did. Then I used the seating chart to take attendance, moving students who had misread it, and writing down nicknames or pronunciations.

I managed this seating chart exercise with a smile and good humor. I gently teased students who ended up in the wrong seat and made fun of myself when I mispronounced their names, but I had now set a tone of productivity from the beginning of class (even before the bell rang), and by establishing where they would sit I also slyly informed them that I was in control.

After taking attendance, I briefly introduced myself and the class expectations. Students need to know what to expect each year and want to know a little about their teachers, but they cannot listen for hours all day, so I kept this short. During this introduction time, I did go over my class rules, again keeping it short. They were simple:

Class Rules

1. Keep the class flowing. If you need to interrupt, wait until an appropriate time.

2. DO NOT make fun of anyone's writing.

3. You may have mints or water, but no food, drinks, or gum in class.

4. DO NOT CHEAT. If I catch you cheating, I reserve the right to embarrass you, give you a zero on the assignment, and call your parents.

5. Watch your language. This is an English class, so look for the word that will not get you into trouble.

I went over these rules quickly and with as much laughter as I could elicit from the class. For rule #2, I would try to find Mr. Popularity, the one who could not stay quiet during class up to that point. I would point him out to the class and say, "If Joe here comes in wearing a plaid shirt and golfing pants with his man-bun dyed pink, he probably wants you to laugh at him. Feel free! He needs you to laugh at him! However, if Joe writes a story that is the worst thing you have ever read, your job is to help him make it better, not to make him feel bad for it."

Students always want to know why they cannot have gum. I told them it is because they leave gum under desks or on the floor, but that is not the real reason. This instead is another lesson my intern supervisor taught me. If I caught them chewing gum, I simply asked them to go throw it in the trash. I tried not to make this a real discipline issue (although if they became defiant, that was a different issue that we will cover later). What I achieved, though, was priceless: students knew I was watching them. They sometimes made it a game among themselves to see how long they could keep gum in their mouths before I caught them (I pretended to be offended by this), but they invariably would tell me by the end of the year that they would never try anything really bad BECAUSE THEY KNEW I WOULD CATCH THEM. So, there you have it, the real reason that my classroom is a gum-free zone: If students knew I saw them chewing gum, then they assumed I could see everything. In the old days, we called it *withitness*.

Since I used only twenty minutes or so on introduction, I still had time to teach – yes, teach – on the first day of school. Those little get-to-know-you activities are fun, but students do them many times in other classes and get bored with them. Again, set the tone. I never wanted students to think of my class as just social time; I wanted them to come in every day expecting to learn something. I have used several first-day lessons. Sometimes I used a game with homonyms and homophones. It includes group work, dictionary work, and writing on the board. Other times, I had them read the name essay from Sandra Cisneros' *The House on Mango Street,* led them to analyze it as a class, and then had them write their own name essays using hers as a model. The idea here is that we learn and work on the first day (the name essay often even became homework, due the next day). The lessons were not difficult, but they set an academic tone for the year.

You may think I have spent a lot of time talking about the first day of school, a honeymoon day that usually has very few behavior issues, but if you wait until you have behavior issues to think about classroom management, you have waited too long. Setting a tone at the beginning that prevents problems is much easier than reacting to problems after they occur. In fact, on the first day of school, in addition to dressing very professionally, I usually wore a red blouse that looked like something a banker would wear, what I called my power colors. As a student, I loved to walk into class on the first day and find a young teacher dressed in hippie-type clothes. That always told me the class would be easy. That, however, was not the impression I wanted my own students to have. Instead, I wore clothes that suggested that I deserved respect.

"No" makes your life easier

Another technique that prevents problems is the word *No.* Young teachers believe that giving in to student requests will make students like them and in turn lead to an easy class. In fact, I sat in on an interview in which a new teacher responded to a question on classroom management by saying that she would make her class like her. After the interview, the hiring committee just laughed. The truth is, the harder you try to make students like you, the less they respect you and the more likely they are to push the boundaries with you.

Do not get me wrong. I am not suggesting that you must be surly and unpleasant, but teenagers are natural lawyers. Every *yes* is an open door to them, and each time you give in to a request, you invite more. Requests for seat changes, reasons to leave your classroom, deadline extensions should be answered with *no*. Occasionally, a student will meet with you in private to give a particularly good reason for a *yes*. Say yes! However, tell the student that she is not to discuss this special privilege with anyone. She will feel honored that you gave in to her, and you will not have lost your edge with the class. Bear in mind, though, that this student now will probably ask you for other exceptions until you finally have to say no.

Parent Contacts

I really hated calling parents. Every time I thought I should call, I came up with lots of reasons to postpone, and I always thought the parent was going to blame me for whatever the problem was. Contacting parents is one of your most effective tools, both for classroom discipline issues and for keeping yourself out of trouble later.

The best advice I ever got was from my college professor in the education department at the University of Tampa. She had taught junior high in the Bronx in the 1970s, so we believed everything she said about classroom management. She said to call parents with good news before you ever have a problem. She was right! I made a point of noticing during the first few weeks of school who my problem children would be and then calling their parents with good news. Sometimes I had to look hard to find something good, but when I did, the parent was on my side. Then later, when I had to call about a problem, the parent did not automatically think that I did not like their child.

My new favorite tech advance is Google Voice. When Covid-19 closed our schools this year, we all got Google Voice numbers so that we could call parents from home without giving out our personal phone numbers. With Google Voice, I discovered I could go online and text (most) parents instead of calling them. I have never had such positive parent responses as I did from this. Somehow, parents do not always answer their phones, or they ignore calls from the school, but they almost always respond to texts! Imagine texting a parent during class to let them know that their son is keeping you from teaching.

goal is to teach. Grab their attention and get back to teaching.

Defiance

What do you do about the student who is spoiling for a fight, the one who came in with a chip on her shoulder and is going to defy you, regardless of what you say? First, do not get drawn into a battle with that student. Your mission is to teach, and every time you get into a battle of wills, you fail in your mission.

Here are conversations that I have had with students, maybe not verbatim, but often enough that they are much the same:

Conversation 1:

"Matt go sit in your assigned seat."

"But why does Kelly…?"

"Don't worry about Kelly; go sit in your assigned seat."

"But can I…?"

"No, Matt, go sit in your assigned seat."

"But why? What did I do?"

"If you need to know why, see me after class and I'll explain it to you. Now move."

Conversation 2:

"Make your choice. Do as I say or take the referral."
Then I keep teaching.

Now other students are looking at me and looking at
him, trying to decide whether to follow suit. I remind
them of the consequences, but do not say exactly what
they will be.

"The rest of you can do the same thing he's doing, but
you have to ask yourself whether you are willing to
suffer the same consequences. And whether your
parents will be happy with those same consequences."

Then I keep teaching.

After the first conversation in class last year, another
student grinned and said, "You don't negotiate, do
you?" In both situations, I have made it clear that the
behavior is not acceptable, but I have also refused to
be drawn into battle. If the student is not endangering
himself or another student, you should not do battle.

This does not mean, however, that there are no
consequences. If the direct instruction is over and the
students are working at their desks, I may go back to
the defiant student to discuss the issue. This has given
him and me time to cool down and talk reasonably.

Do not discount this cool-down time! You probably already understand that adolescent hormones and lack of development cause them to say and do things they later regret, but the same is also true of you, the adult. In the heat of anger, with thirty sets of eyes on you, you will feel backed into a corner, ready to threaten all kinds of consequences. Do not have that conversation while your face is still hot.

However, once you have cooled down and the class is focused on their assignment, you can have a civil conversation. If this behavior is out of the ordinary, you can ask what is going on. Remind the student that this is not like him and that you are concerned. In this case, you still need to issue consequences, but it can be something as mild as a lunch detention.

On the other hand, if this is recurrent behavior, you can still have the conversation, but you will point out that this happens too often. Point out also the effect of this defiance on the rest of the class. You can tell the student what the consequence will be but tell him you would rather see him change his behavior than for you to have to continue addressing it.

Either way, DO NOT LECTURE. Speak for a minute, but do not let your conversation be part of the punishment.

Everything so far has been about students who are being mildly defiant. However, if a student gets out of control or prevents you from teaching, it is time to call for help. Get on the phone and ask someone from the office to come escort this student from class. If necessary, enlist the help of the teacher next door to you. Keep in mind, though, that this is a last resort only when the student is preventing you from teaching.

Refusal to Work

When a student puts his head down and just refuses to work on an assignment, your first step is diagnosis. Is this defiance? Does he not understand but does not want to look stupid? (Many students would rather be bad than stupid.) It may be that you will never know why a student refuses.

If the issue is defiance—he is just angry at you and the world—then treat it as we discussed in the defiance section. Another trick I have used very successfully is to call home right then and there. Start by telling the student that he is welcome to take a zero on the assignment, but you must have his mother's permission first. Often just the threat of calling home is enough to spur them on. If that does not work, call. Right there, in front of the whole class, call the parent.

"Hi, this is Mrs. Smith. I am Cole's English teacher. Cole is in my class right now, but he says he will not do the assignment. I told him he could take the zero, but he needed your permission first. Would you like to talk to him?" They ALWAYS want to talk to their child.

This has worked for me every time except one. That parent made excuses for her son and said it was fine for him to take the zero. That is OK! Even if this strategy did not get that student back to work, it certainly got the rest of the class back on task. They did not want to be the next phone call.

Dennis

Dennis was his own special case. For the whole year, he did zero assignments and refused to take any assessments. He was never disrespectful, but he also did not struggle with the subject. In fact, when we read out loud or had class discussion, he participated. He just would not do anything written. I will admit that I never found out why. My attempts at parent contacts were completely unsuccessful, and even the school counselor and social worker were no help.

Then one day Tariq joined our class. He spoke English, but badly, and he and Dennis sat near each other. It had always been my habit to pair ESL students with successful students, but Tariq got along well with Dennis, so I paired them up. Dennis became his tutor in class. They did every single assignment together, but Dennis never wrote a word. I made a deal with him. If he would help Tariq with his assignments, I would give Dennis whatever grade Tariq earned—including tests and quizzes. Dennis agreed.

I will not say that this turned Dennis' life around. He passed one quarter of the year, which means he ended the year with a failing grade. However, I can say that he learned the material. As he tutored Tariq, he processed the information himself, and both students were the better for their partnership.

Other Things to Try

Sometimes a student is just fidgety, looking for trouble, but not really doing anything bad. If you notice that he is antsy early, you have a chance to stop a little problem before it becomes a big one.

My favorite trick was to send students like this on a faux errand. If he really is antsy, he probably will be happy for any excuse to get out of your classroom, so he will not argue about doing you a favor.

Write a note to another teacher you trust. In it, say something like, "Luke needed a break from my class. Please take a minute to think, write something on this paper, and then send him back to me with your 'response.'" Then staple the paper so Luke cannot see what you have written and send him on his way.

Most likely, when Luke returns to class, he will have expended all that energy that was causing his problem and can then get back to learning. Plus, he got some extra attention from you.

Sending student out of class

When students have gone beyond being merely fidgety to being disruptive, but not enough that calls for strong disciplinary action like a detention or referral, you could send them to another room. Never just tell a student to leave your room. When you do that, you have given him permission to go anywhere, and you are no longer doing your job of supervising him.

Instead, pre-arrange with another teacher to be each other's holding rooms. I always preferred to send troublesome students to a class full of seniors or to an AP class. For some reason, misbehaving students, especially younger ones, get really embarrassed to be in a class full of students who are paying attention and working.

Send them with something to do. If you have assigned work, you can send them with their assignment. You might also create a form to send with them that asks them to explain why they were sent out and what they should do in the future to avoid your corrective action.

Tell the student when he should return and watch from the open door to ensure that the student goes where you sent him. If he does not, this should be an automatic referral to the office for refusing to comply with your disciplinary action.

Make sure you document this action and contact their parents. Then if you do have to write a referral in the future, you can show that you have tried many other strategies first.

In Conclusion

Classroom management is more than discipline. It is being organized from the beginning so that your students do not have time to get into trouble.

Set the standard. You are the adult in the room and set the standard for behavior. First as a student and then as a teacher, I had a hard time respecting instructors who eat in class or even who chew gum while they teach. And stay off your phone! As we are adults and sometimes spouses and parents, we do get texts that matter, and sometimes we get phone calls that we have to take immediately, but do you really want to take out your phone in front of your class every time you get a notification? I finally got a smart watch for school so that when I got a call or text, I could glance at my wrist to see whether it was important rather than pulling out my phone.

TEACH. Your mission is to teach your class, not to lecture. Do not make a fuss about behavior. Address it and then go right back to teaching.

Chapter Three

Organization

When I started teaching, I was the least organized person I knew. Like most disorganized people, I would say that I never lost anything, that I knew what was in every pile on my desk, but being disorganized made teaching incredibly stressful.

Then I married the most organized person I ever met, and I started to learn from him. Now, because it does not come naturally to me, I am able to help other teachers to organize their classrooms. If I can learn the skill, anyone can.

Time Management

Whatever is on our mind right now is what we want to think about. I just collected a set of tests or essays, and I really want to see how my students did. Or I have a great idea for the next unit and want to get started planning it. However, living that way can make you terribly underprepared for the next hour or the next day.

Organize your planning time this way:

1. What do I need to do in order to teach today? Have I planned for the first class I teach? Have I copied everything I need to teach with? Have I checked my presentation slides? Do I have my textbooks where

kids can access them? Do I have my teacher's edition accessible and annotated? I ask these questions for each class I must teach, particularly since most teachers have more than one prep.

2. Check your calendar. Do you have any meetings today after school or during your planning period? What do you need to prepare for that meeting? Do you need to print a student's grades or gather work samples to take with you?

3. What do I need to do for tomorrow? Have I planned everything for tomorrow's classes? Have I copied everything for tomorrow? Is there anything I need to grade so that I can hand it back tomorrow?

4. How close am I to the end of the unit I am teaching? If it ends within the next two or three days, I should start planning the next unit now. If I have more than three days, I need to jot down some ideas in case I need to gather materials, but I probably should grade papers now instead.

5. Do not forget to keep a to-do list handy. You will fill it up and check it off throughout the day.

Planning is always more fun than grading, and we are tempted to put all our energy into it, but be careful not to let the ungraded papers pile up. See the chapter on grading for tips to make it go faster, but students deserve to get their work back in a timely manner.

Calendars

It might seem odd for me to give you advice on calendars. After all, you have graduated with at least a four-year degree and have been managing your calendar successfully all this time. However, so much happens so quickly during the school day, that you need a calendar you can see at a glance. Most high schools still receive printed desk calendars either from the teacher's union or from military recruiters. If nothing else, you can print your online calendar each month. My point here is that you will have things pop up regularly—IEP meetings, professional-development plan due dates, homecoming, underclassman picture day, the day you plan to collect research papers—all of these need to end up on your calendar, the calendar you see all the time. That way, when you must make an on-the-spot decision about a date, you do not have to open your computer to figure it out. Being able to see everything briefly helps you to keep your head straight.

I ended up using both, the desk calendar and the online calendar. Online, I subscribed to the school calendar and added my own appointments. I liked getting pop-up reminders of meetings and such. However, I kept the desk calendar right under my computer and looked at it many times throughout the day. Then when a student asked to come in at lunch on a particular day for help, I knew immediately whether I had a lunchtime meeting that day (which is not as rare as you hope it is). When a colleague asked when I would be done with the novels (yes, calling me on the phone during class to ask this question) I could glance at my desk calendar and tell her which day I had scheduled the test. Knowing when homecoming and prom were kept me from making impossible due dates for my upper classmen. If this is your first-year teaching, try keeping a paper calendar. You can always tweak your style next year.

Working at home

Facebook is full of teachers complaining about how much time they spend grading and planning at home. I often saw my colleagues dragging home rolling carts full of papers to grade, and then dragging them back again the next day, having never touched them.

Exceedingly early in my career, a teacher near retirement age told me that she was not paid to work from home and would not sacrifice her family to her job. That stuck with me.

During your first three years of teaching, you are doing many things for the first time. Everything takes longer than it should, and you really cannot get everything done at work. You will spend several hours each evening planning and grading. However, that cannot go on forever. Learn to use your planning time efficiently. Grade when students are working independently. Try very hard not to take work home with you. By the end of my career, the only time I took work home was when I had large projects like research papers. Sometimes I took essays home to grade, since they required more undivided attention than I could give at school. Otherwise, work stayed at work.

Classroom layout

The first time you walk into your classroom is exciting – and daunting! It is probably cluttered from the summer custodial work and filled with stuff the previous teacher left behind, and because you are new to the school, it is probably also tiny and run-down. After all, when the good classroom opened last year, the senior teachers all petitioned for it before you ever got hired!

So where do you start? You will spend more waking hours in this room as you will your own house, so make it your own. I have always found this task overwhelming—where do I start first? Make a to-do list on the board! This is not the order in which you must do things, but these need to get done.

1. **Clean it up.** Get cleaning supplies from the custodians or bring in your own if you are allowed. Look around the room; you may find cleaning supplies the other teacher left behind. Clear away the dust and the cobwebs that inevitably gather. Your students do not want to walk into the dungeon.

2. **Organize the desks last.** You are going to move books from one side of the room to the other (several times) and you do not want to have to push desks out of the way constantly.

3. Clear a **workspace** for yourself. You are going to use your desk the most during your planning before school starts.

4. Figure out the **physical layout** of your room. Consider the following:

a. Where do you want your desk? Will you teach near your desk? If so, you need it near the front center of the room. I often kept mine in a front corner so I could access it easily but taught from a podium. However, in the past I have chosen to keep it in the back corner so I could see students easily when they were working. Keeping my desk in the back corner, however, meant that I had to be particularly prepared in having all materials I needed for teaching on a small table next to my podium.

b. Something else to consider is your teacher desk's relationship to the door. Keeping school violence in mind, I wanted to be able to see through my door window when I was at my desk. It helped me to stay aware of who was walking past my classroom, especially when I was alone during planning (since I did not sit much at my desk during class). Other teachers prefer to keep their desk hidden from view of the door or window so that they can work during their planning period or eat a quiet lunch without being interrupted.

c. Where will students get materials? You will likely have class sets of books for students to use. Where will those be? You may have bookshelves for them: make sure students can get to those bookshelves easily. You may also keep them stored in cabinets. Do you want students to be able to go into those cabinets? Are there other materials in cabinets you do not want them to access?

d. Do you have places that need to be blocked off? If you are in an older school, you may have a room in which one wall is a curtain. Ask the teacher on the other side of that curtain whether much noise gets through. Consider putting your bookshelves and filing cabinets against the curtain or adjoining wall as noise control. Then look for places where students might go to hide. Yes, we are talking about high school, but some kid is going to try to hide from you behind your cabinets and write all over them. Use your bookshelves and filing cabinets strategically.

e. Other areas for student materials will include the pencil sharpener, stapler, hole punch, spare pencils, spare notebook paper, *etc.* I do not like students taking those things from my desk, so I set up an area on the counter and make it attractive. You also want this far from the front of the room. If a student needs a pencil while I am teaching, I would rather he did not make a show of it in front of the rest of the class (and he will!).

f. Where will students turn in papers? When I inherited a classroom fifteen years ago, the previous teacher had left a wire basket on the desk. It was ugly, but it was deep and wide and could hold probably two reams of paper. This became my student turn-in basket, and for fifteen years it sat on the right corner of my desk. Students always knew to turn all their work into that basket, and I never lost a paper. Do not underestimate the value of a single turn-in spot. Students will just lay work on your desk if you do not tell them where to do it, and—trust me on this—you will lose something. At the end of each day (if possible, at the end of the period, but usually not) I would go through the basket and sort out assignments, taking out any makeup work. This was truly a life saver!

g. Now you can organize your student desks. You can choose to place them in rows, in groups, in a semicircle, or in some other creative arrangement. The plan for collaborative work often tempts teachers into organizing their desks into collaborative groups from the start of the year. However, if you are new to teaching, I advise you to start with rows. Yes, it may seem old-fashioned and authoritarian, but any arrangement other than rows sets you up for discipline issues that you may not yet have the experience to handle. When students can see each other face-to-face, they will talk. They cannot help it! And remember that many of these students have been in school together since elementary and are long-time friends (or enemies), so their focus will be on each other and not on what you want to teach them.

h. Start them off in rows. Then when you use collaborative groups later, you can allow them to push their desks together for a time and then straighten the rows again at the end of the period. ***Classroom Management Tip*** Having students straighten the rows at the end of a period when they've been working collaboratively helps you to reestablish your position as teacher, gives you a chance to give any last-minute reminders about homework, upcoming tests, *etc.*, and takes away that dangerous free time when conflicts are most likely to occur.

i. Do not forget to give yourself room to walk, not just between the rows, but in the back of the room. You really need to be able to see your students from the back when they cannot see that you are watching them.

All Those Little Things

School happens fast! You will be exhausted at the end of each day because you have been moving and thinking at a sprint all day. No matter how prepared you are, as soon as students come into the room, they will inundate you with information and requests: "Did I miss anything yesterday?" (as if the answer might be no). "Can I get make-up work from my absence?" "Here's my make-up work from when I was out all last week." "I have a note to turn in to the office. Can I go now?" "Can I go to the restroom before class starts?" "I have a migraine today. Can I just keep my head down all period?"

All those little things can add up to an overwhelming mountain if you do not get a handle on it quickly. Your desk will end up covered in make-up work, notes to the office, notes from parents, and you will lose something – probably something important.

Here are some ways I have learned to deal with the mountain:

• **Color-coded folders**. Get yourself a box of colored file folders and label them: Grade now, Make-up Work, Office, Copy. You may find that you need other categories, but these will get you started. When you have things to go to the office—student absent notes, all the first-week forms that students turn in, the forms the principal's secretary needs by the end of the week—put them into your office folder. Then, every time you leave your classroom, grab that orange folder and you will never forget to turn stuff in. When you do your lesson planning and need to make copies later, put it into your green copy folder. Then it will not be just sitting in a pile on your desk waiting to get accidentally knocked into the trash can. If you have a code for the copier, write that inside the folder.

• **Papers to Return.** I found that stacked trays are the easiest way to get papers back to students. After I graded and recorded assignments, I put them into the tray labeled with that class period. When forms came from the office for me to give to students, I also added those to the class tray. When the guidance counselor emailed me that she needed to see a student during third period, I printed the email and put it into the third-period bin. When the office sent out a pack of letters that my seventh-period students needed to take home, it went into the seventh-period bin. Then while students were completing a warm-up exercise or were working after my lesson, I returned whatever was in the tray.

• **Make-up work.** One of the neatest tricks I learned is to do this: at the end of the day (or at the end of the period if you have time) put the names of absent students on blank worksheets from that day. Then those sheets also go into the tray of work to return. If I gave instructions on the board, I typed those instructions and printed them with absentee names on top as well. The more you can do for yourself ahead of time, the easier your day goes. Some teachers like to keep a place for makeup work that students can access independently. They create a notebook and put into it a printed copy of the day's notes and whatever assignments absent students need to complete. However, I have found that few students will use that system the way it is intended. Maybe my method enables dependency over independence, but I got tired of reminding students about the makeup notebook even late in the year.

• **Printed Rosters.** I started teaching before teachers had computers, so I have always been accustomed to keeping my grades and attendance on paper. Even after we started keeping computerized grades and attendance, things often went wrong. Teachers in the early years sometimes lost weeks of grades when the server crashed. That is less likely to happen now, but keeping paper grades has helped me in several ways. When I printed my blank roster, it was alphabetical. When I recorded graded papers, I wrote the scores on the paper roster and then entered them into my computerized gradebook. Entering the grades alphabetically saved me the time of scrolling up and down to find the right name, especially frustrating in large classes. Having a written copy also gave me a backup when I typed in the wrong score, 10% instead of 100% for instance. Anytime I could avoid looking foolish in front of my class, I was happy. I also marked my attendance on a separate printed roster. Most of the time I used my computer at the beginning of the period to project the warm-up or for the presentation during my lesson, so I could not also use the computer to take attendance. I wrote it on the printed roster and entered it later while students were working.

- **Notebooks/clipboards.** In addition to colored file folders, I am also a fan of notebooks and clipboards. I kept my attendance in a notebook labeled as such so that I could find it easily. It was also nice for my substitutes to be able to find my attendance folder easily. More importantly to me, though, were my two clipboards. On one I kept my printed roster for grades. I constantly picked up that one since I assigned many practices in a lesson. Sometimes I also made notes to myself about participation. The other clipboard had my seating charts. Our computerized gradebook allowed us to print a seating chart with pictures. Since I have always struggled to learn students' names, I carried this seating chart clipboard around with me all the time. Keeping both charts on clipboards kept me from losing the paper in a pile on my desk; I just looked for the clipboard!

Organize your class time

I like structure, and so did my students. One of the most consistent compliments I received from students each year is that they always knew what to expect and where to find it. On the white board in my classroom—every day—students knew they could find a list of due dates and an agenda.

Students appreciate the list of **due dates**. One thing you will notice with high-school students, especially upper classmen, is that they are busy people! They often have sports and clubs after school, and many of them also work. It is hard on students to give them a large assignment today that is due tomorrow. In fact, I would tell them this during my introduction on the first day: "I know you are busy people (and if you are in my AP class, you are probably in other AP classes as well). Therefore, I will TRY not to give you homework today that is due tomorrow. I will try to give you as much notice as possible so that you can manage your own time and get it done when you can concentrate on it. However, that means that I must be strict about due dates. If I give you several days to complete an assignment, I expect you to have it here on time." They always agreed that this was a fair exchange.

That did not mean I never gave last-minute homework! Sometimes we just cannot finish something in class, and they must finish it at home. That circumstance should not require more than ten minutes at home, though.

Having the due dates on the board also protected me. I could not always remember to tell kids that their vocabulary sentences were due tomorrow. However, once the pattern was established, they reminded each other!

Do not worry that your due dates might have to change after you have written them on the board. Many times, one circumstance or the other caused me to have to change a due date. Just point it out to your students! Most of the time, you are telling them they have more time than you first anticipated anyway, so they are happy to get the news. The point is that everyone wants to be informed and to know what to expect. I wanted my principal to tell me what was coming up, and I extended the same courtesy to my students.

Some days the **agenda on the board** was more specific than others, but it was always in the same place. The agenda helped me to stay on track. As I finished one thing, I pointed to the agenda and said we were done with that and were now moving on to the next point. This really helped my ADHD kids. They could track with me, and they also could see that we were that much closer to the end. Sometimes we all need to see the light at the end of the tunnel!

My class always began with warm-up **activity**. Since I taught English, it was often a grammar or vocabulary exercise, but I also liked warm-up time for reviewing yesterday's lesson. In years when I needed to hold kids accountable, I would collect warm-ups each week for a weekly grade. I hesitate to admit to you that during my first year of teaching, I collected them daily for a grade. I spent way more time grading warm-ups than they were worth, and I learned that lesson quickly. Later, I learned to use Kahoot and other online tools for warmups. Whatever you do, make sure it is short – no more than ten minutes – and make sure it is academic. If a parent or your principal should ask you its purpose, you must be able to justify it.

Warm-up time is also when I took attendance and handed back papers. If you have trouble with students being tardy, you can even use this time to motivate them to be on time.

After the warm-up, I reminded them of upcoming due dates or tests and then got right into the lesson. Some teachers love to hear themselves talk, but I married a man with ADHD and learned early to recognize the glaze in his eyes. For that reason, most of my lessons lasted five to ten minutes before I had students do something. I may have had several of those cycles of teaching and activity during the period, but most high-school students cannot listen for long. After a while, I learned to imbed those practices into my lesson, so one presentation might last several days, moving from teaching to activity to feedback and then back to teaching again.

In Conclusion

Students appreciate organization, especially when they themselves are disorganized. Keep your classroom organized, and your stress will decrease. Keep your lessons short, and transition often during class. You and your students will be amazed constantly by how quickly that hour flies by!

Chapter Four

Safety

School today is quite different from when I was a student. Although school violence did not start at Columbine, that event sticks out to me as the beginning of a trend. The year after the Columbine shooting, I got a new student in my class who had attended one of Columbine High School's nearby rivals. She told us how much our school was like Columbine in its normal-ness. Her point was that nobody could have anticipated what happened there. Since then, we have had many more incidents punctuated by those that will stick out as especially heinous: Sandy Hook left me its image of elementary students huddled in a corner with their teacher trying to protect them with her body; Parkland was in south Florida, while my school was in central Florida. As I listened to Parkland teachers tell of trying to get students out of the stairwells and halls safely into their classrooms, I couldn't help glancing out my door at the stairwell directly across the hall and wondering how successful I could be at protecting my own students.

My husband spent much of his law-enforcement career as a school resource officer and helped to develop the first emergency plan for our school district. Additionally, he and I met in the Army Reserve Military Police Corps (I spent the first half of my teaching career as a weekend warrior) so we spent many hours over the years talking about what-if situations. I won't discuss the politics of school safety; whether teachers should be armed, whether we should have more SROs in schools, whether we should spend more money on mental health counseling or education—these are policies that are way above my pay grade as a classroom teacher. What I can tell you is what I have done as a result of my long discussions with my husband as well as my own experience and research.

Be Aware

The most important thing you can do to ensure your safety and the safety of your students is to be aware of your surroundings. Nothing annoyed me more at school than to see students walking around with both ears clogged by earbuds, looking down at their phones. I could yell their names while standing in front of them, and they would not hear me. How in the world would they hear a shooter or notice any danger? At the beginning of our first safety drill of the year, I had this discussion with each class: You have five senses. Sight and sound alert you to long-distance danger. Smell might alert you to smoke. By the time you feel or taste danger, it is too close for you to avoid it. So why would you eliminate the only two senses that can notify you and give you time to react to danger?

As a teacher, you are probably not walking around wearing earbuds, but do you walk the hall with your face in your phone? In your classroom, are you aware when something is out of place? This goes back to the chapter on organization; keep your classroom organized so that it always looks the same, and then you will notice when it is not the same. What about when your students are "off"? If a normally chatty kid puts his head down, notice it. Quietly asking a kid, "Everything OK today?" lets a sad kid know that you care and lets an angry kid know that you noticed. Awareness is the first step in preventing problems.

Do you have a way to note when a student from another class comes into your room? Kids like to play tricks, and occasionally I noticed a strange student sitting in a desk next to his friend, grinning up at me as he waited for me to see him. This should not have happened! How did he get into my room without my noticing? As teachers, we get so busy dealing with everything at once, that we forget to pay attention to the door opening and closing. Pay attention to that noise. If you are working with a student or a group, you may not see your door opening, so take note of the sound it makes when it closes and look up every time you hear that sound. Most of the time, it will be a kid returning from the restroom or whatever pass you sent him on, but sometimes it will be your principal coming in to observe you. You will look much more with-it if you notice and quietly acknowledge her presence, much more than if she stands there ten minutes before you jump out of your skin at the sight of her.

Being alert to your surroundings is the first step in protecting yourself and your students.

Have a plan

After being aware, having a plan the second step you need to prepare for any dangerous situation. Play what-if games with yourself. What if a fight breaks out in my room? What if a kid has a seizure? What if I hear gun shots outside? What if the secretary announces a lockdown for a real gunman? What if someone bursts into my room to harm my students?

Does this sound paranoid? Maybe, but I would rather have a plan that I never needed than to need a plan and not have it. Here is my answer for each of these, but you will have to tailor your plan to your situation.

Fights

In thirty years of teaching, I never had to break up a fight. Maybe I was lucky, but part of that luck was seeing that a fight was going to happen and stepping in to prevent it first. I do not necessarily recommend getting between two boys who are swinging on each other, but most kids look for an excuse NOT to fight. Shout STOP in your most commanding teacher voice. Push a desk between them. Tell their friends to take them away from each other—this is amazingly effective. Students who fight usually have friends who will try to talk them down. Make use of these friends to help you get the combatants far apart.

Medical Emergencies

You cannot predict every medical emergency that might happen. I have had three different students have seizures during class, and each of them was a different situation. The first thing you can do to prepare is to make a phone cheat sheet. Our school's directory was four pages long, so I typed out the numbers I wanted at my fingertips and posted it next to my phone. These numbers included the direct lines to the clinic, SRO, principal's secretary, discipline assistant, guidance counselors, ESE support person, and department head. You may notice other numbers you call regularly that you want to add.

During the first month of school, you will probably receive a deluge of Emergency Health Plans for students. Unfortunately, the sheer volume of information makes it difficult to process any of it. Compound that problem with the requirement that you keep student information confidential. So now you must figure out a way to have this information easily accessible when you need it without making it visible to other students.

Since I am old school, I kept a fat notebook of alphabetized student information in the very front of my file cabinet. When I got these Health Plans, I printed them and put them into the notebook for easy access. When you print them, you can tell which issues are minor and which are major. Asthma, for instance, is a bigger issue to an elementary teacher than to a high school teacher. By this time, the student knows much more about how to handle their asthma than you do. So, as I looked through the plans, I paid attention to the issues that might be a problem in class and noted them on my attendance chart (in my own secret code). Then some time during the first month of school, I would quietly take that student aside and ask about the medical issue so that I could be prepared if something were to happen. This conversation had the extra benefit of helping me to remember this student's issue since I struggled to recall all the important details of all 150 new students in my class.

School Violence

Fights and medical emergencies are likely to happen; school shootings are far less likely, but awareness and planning are still the best way to prepare for them. Start with your school's emergency plan. Most likely, your school has a checklist of what you should do in the event of a violent threat, and that is where you start. Most schools now have plans for both locking down and evacuating, depending on where you are in relation to the threat. While there is no threat, while you can think clearly, is the time to decide what you feel safest doing. If you know a threat is on the other side of the school, you may decide your students will be safest in running away from campus. On the other hand, if you do not know where the threat is, you will decide to lock down your classroom. Plan for both. I cannot give much advice for evacuation since your school's physical location will determine most of those decisions; however, here are some considerations for lockdown:

Cover and Concealment

Many people use these terms interchangeably, but they are not the same. Items that give cover will protect you from gunfire. Items that provide concealment will hide you but will not protect you. For instance, during a lockdown, students may choose to hide in cabinets, in a storeroom, or behind a bookshelf. Those items will keep you from being seen but will not stop bullets. I had a storeroom in my last classroom and decided that it would be a good place for my students to gather during a lockdown. However, drywall does not provide protective cover. To add protection for my students, I moved file cabinets and bookshelves to that wall. While none of those alone would be enough, adding more layers between my students and a threat gave them that much more protection.

What you practice is what you will do

During drills, students will talk, giggle, text, play games, watch videos, do anything except take the drill seriously. Remind students that what they do during a drill is what they will do when it really happens. Turn the lights off and cover the windows (I used a black curtain with magnets sewn into the top to cover my large classroom window) and then BE QUIET!

Then I asked students the same thing you should ask yourself: Would you rather hide or fight? Look, there is no judgement here. You need to know ahead of time, though. If someone bursts into your room, will you fight or hide? If you know you cannot fight back, then get out of the way. Show your students where to hide, how to get behind heavy teacher desks, how to put their bookbags between themselves and the threat.

Maybe you, like me, are a fighter. After the stories of Sandy Hook, I adopted the mindset that if I must die in a school shooting, I would die fighting back. A bad guy might do damage to my students, but I would certainly make him pay dearly. Look around your classroom at all the weapons at your disposal. My students got a kick out of the idea that they could throw a textbook, a stapler, or even a desk at someone and do some real damage. Most teachers even have a small toolkit in their rooms. I always kept a little screwdriver in my desk drawer, but I added a hammer to use, as necessary. Do you know how to use the fire extinguisher in your room? Lift it off its hook and notice how heavy it is. In the right hands, it would do some real damage before you even sprayed it!

My favorite secret weapon is wasp spray. Do you know that a can of wasp spray can shoot a stream over ten feet? Of course, you will not let your student near it, and you will not even tell them you have it. You may prepare your students well during a drill, but you will not tell them about the hammer or the wasp spray until they need to use it. Do some research. I found many web sites dedicated to protecting yourself in an office environment.

Does this sound paranoid to you? During thirty years of teaching, I did not experience any school shootings, but I have seen fights and medical emergencies. However, I do not regret being prepared.

Chapter Five

Administration

In thirty years, I worked at five schools under eight principals. One of those principals always reminded me of an Old-Testament king: whenever I walked into his office, I wondered whether he would lower his scepter to admit me or call his guards to have my head chopped off! Much as he scared me, the school was excellent under his leadership. Another principal I worked for was fired for reasons I will not go into here. The point is that during your career you will have to work for many different leaders, each with his or her own style.

Keep in mind that principals and assistant principals start their careers as teachers, but the skills for each job are vastly different. In our district, anyone with three years of teaching experience and the required degrees can apply to be an assistant principal. That means that you could end up working for someone with the experience of a fourth-year teacher! I have seen excellent teachers with more than a decade of experience become terrible administrators, and I have also seen young coaches or behavior specialists with little classroom experience become excellent principals. Their job is less about being an educator than it is about being a good manager of adults.

Your principal is not your friend.

The hardest lesson for most teachers to learn is that no matter how friendly or personable, **your principal is not your friend**. Your principal has a school to run, and her goal is to make that school successful. To do so, she will use all the information and tools she has, even those she acquired in friendship. When you tell her about your health issues and how they keep you from dealing well with stress, she may decide that you are not as well equipped to teach an AP class as a healthier peer. If she knows that you are often absent because of your young children, she may decide to assign you co-teach classes all day just so she does not have to hire substitutes for you as often.

Please do not think that I am judging principals harshly or calling them mercenary. They have an exceedingly difficult job to do and must do what is best for their school. However, no matter how friendly you are with your administration, keep in mind that running the school—not your friendship—is their priority.

What to do when they do not support you

Sometimes we just do not click with our principal. You may feel a lack of support for teachers in general, or maybe you think she does not like you. You may decide just to keep your head down and wait her out. After all, teachers often spend more of their career at a single school than principals do. During the term of one principal, I kept reminding myself: "I was here when she arrived; I'll be here when she leaves." It worked. I

68

kept my head down, did not volunteer for anything, and just waited her out. In that case, keeping a low profile kept me off her radar, even when other teachers were not so lucky. When the problem becomes more personal and it is you she does not like, you may need to be more active.

Step One: Self-assessment

The first thing I tell new teachers to do is to look at yourself. Does your principal have a legitimate beef with you? We all get defensive when we feel attacked, but if two or three people say the same thing about you, it might be true. Are you constantly late to school or absent on Mondays? Do you often forget to submit attendance, lesson plans, accommodation logs—do you need to be reminded or even nagged to get your paperwork in on time? Do parents or peers complain to your principal about you? Are you—gulp—confrontational or difficult to work with? A principal might consider one complaint about you as just the cost of doing business, but multiple complaints suggest that the problem is with you, not the complainers.

If you complete this self-assessment and discover that you have indeed given your principal a reason to distrust or to lack confidence in you, move on to step two. If, however, you decide after honest reflection that the problem is hers and not yours, still move on to step two.

Step Two: Document

If you have a principal who does not like you, you can be sure that your principal is documenting everything you do: every time you are late, every deadline you miss, every complaint. Even if you are being paranoid, you need to believe this is true. Knowing that you are under observation will make you more careful to do things the right way; when you get complacent you will let things slide. This means, however, that you should also document everything. Keep all your emails in a "Saved Emails" folder. Keep records of all parent contacts (you should do this anyway) with the date, time, to whom you spoke, and the highlights of the conversation. This is one reason I prefer text or email contacts with parents: all that information is in writing. Keep a record of when you submit paperwork and to whom—you can do this easily by submitting documents through email.

Jason was an ESE student in my freshman class, and I liked him. He struggled with everything—and I do mean everything—I assigned him, but he came in at lunch for extra help, and his mom was an active participant in his education. I really appreciated being able to call his mom and explain what we were doing in class because she always said she would continue to work with him at home. Then we discovered that Jason's mom used her friendliness to make teachers relax around her. She used everything we said in her lawsuit against the school. She moved her ESE children from school to school, waited for children to struggle, and then sued the schools.

Although this is not an example of a difficult principal, Jason's mom is an example of someone who really was out to get us, and she taught me the importance of documenting everything. Want to know which teacher never had a problem with her? It was Jason's reading teacher, the one who had a piece of paper for every single assignment Jason had completed. Jason's case was one of the most stressful years at our school, but we all became better teachers for it. Dealing with his mom taught all of us to break everything down into its basic parts and how to give a rationale for everything we did.

Step Three: Take their advice

If you think your principal does not like you, your first instinct is probably to be defensive. You will mentally come up with all the reasons she is wrong about you, but this attitude will not help your situation at all. The better approach is humility. Ask her how you can improve and take notes. Do not be afraid to ask! Even if your principal really is being unreasonable, your efforts to improve will help your case.

Invite more experienced teachers into your classroom to observe your teaching and to help you improve. Those teachers should also inform your principal that they are helping you—without telling her anything that they observe or giving any details.

I have done this many times for new teachers. My method is to let the principal know that I intend to observe the new teacher but not the reasons. I even ask the principal to provide coverage for my class while I observe. Because the principal wants to be doing everything possible to help the new teacher, I have never seen this request turned down. Then I take copious notes during my observation and give them to the new teacher in writing. However, I never tell the principal what I observed; that is between me and the new teacher.

And do not forget document everything.

Step Four: Approach with solutions, not with problems.

One of the most important lessons I learned in JROTC (back in the stone age, when I was in high school) was that when I had a problem I should think of the best solution and then approach my leadership with that solution. This lesson served me well in teaching, because, as I said before, principals must worry about the whole school, not just me. Therefore, whenever I had a situation that I wanted the principal to handle for me, I always tried to form it in ways that would help the school and not just myself, even if I was being selfish. For instance, when a great classroom opened, and I knew they were considering who should get it, I made my pitch. I offered to give up some honors classes in exchange for more ESE co-teach classes since that room had an area for group work. I offered to store the freshman novels since that room had more storage than most freshman classrooms. I made giving me that room a solution to two of the principal's problems instead of making it about my preference.

In another situation, a new principal wanted our school to transition from an ESE co-teach model to a dual-certification model. This change was stressful for everyone who was accustomed to having a second teacher in the classroom because it meant the basic-education teacher's having to do all the work alone. However, it was clear that our principal wanted this change to happen, despite her making it sound like a choice at first. Instead of fighting the transition, my colleague and I asked her for a meeting. We proposed spending a day at a nearby school that had already made this transition and finding out from them what worked and what did not. We told her that we wanted to learn from others instead of inventing it ourselves so that we could make the transition more smoothly. Of course, she said yes! We did not tell her all the problems we saw with the program; instead, we offered her a solution.

This attitude has worked for me in other situations. School systems are all about change. Every time a new superintendent takes office, every time a new principal assumes leadership, they want to make their mark. That means change. You do not have to embrace every new idea, but sometimes the best way to deal with change is to get in on the planning. At least then you can have some say on how those new ideas are implemented.

Chapter Six

Bits of Extraneous Advice

Do one thing and do it well.

Like many new teachers, I tried to make myself indispensable during my first few years. In addition to teaching, I coached a sport, sponsored a class, sponsored a club, and directed a school play. After all, most of us get through college on extraordinarily little sleep, so that pattern was easy to continue when I started teaching. However, none of these activities made me indispensable, but they did make me tired. Finally, my husband asked me to choose one thing and let the rest go.

Taking my husband's advice was one of my smartest career moves. I did not quit doing everything, but I did cut back to one extra-curricular activity. When I did that, I quit dreading that after-school time and started enjoying it. My lesson plans became more creative. I graded and returned assignments faster. I became a stronger teacher.

Most of us became teachers because we enjoyed school, and not just the academics. We looked forward to being some student's role model, the coach who saved the day, the director who discovered a student's latent talent. You can still be that, but remember what you were hired to do: teach your classes. Some teachers get so caught up in their extra-curricular activities that they neglect their primary job of teaching. Choose one activity outside your classroom that you can really enjoy and do it well.

Extra-curricular

Your relationship with students during extra-curricular activities is different from in the classroom. You get more opportunities to know them as people—and for them to know you as well. Do not ever forget, though, that you are still the teacher, the responsible adult in the room. You may be twenty-two years old with a group of kids who could be your younger siblings, but you are still the adult.

My most embarrassing moment came when I forgot this lesson. At age twenty-five, I was directing the school's annual prom fashion show, made up of juniors and seniors. This was the same year that I directed the school play and sponsored a club, so I was stretched thin, I was tired, and I did not always make good decisions. The show, however, went well; I was organized and had timed it so well that we were ending a little early. A couple of boys asked if they could go out on stage and ham it up to fill the empty time. I said no at first, but they hounded me. Feeling high from my success, I gave in. They went out on stage and started a striptease—not all the way, of course, just acting the part—in front of the whole school, my principal, and the press who were there to cover the fashion show!

When I entered the principal's office to face the music, there sat those three boys. The principal said they had told him I insisted that they do it. I responded no, but I had given them permission. That was not the only time that students got me to say yes to something and then threw me under the bus for it, but that was the worst time.

Students will always let you take the fall for them. Why? Because it is safer that way for them. They will lie to their parents and get you into trouble if it means that they will stay out of trouble. They do not do this because they hate you but because they are in a panic and are looking for the quickest way out. Keep in mind that every time you say Yes to a student, you must be able to justify your reason to your principal and to their parents.

Eat well.

You will make hundreds of decisions each day in class and log thousands of steps on your smartwatch, and at the end of the day, you will be exhausted.

Too many young teachers roll out of bed and run to school with only a cup of coffee in their stomachs. Then they scarf down lunch if they have time—or worse, they do not have time for lunch, so they snack all day. Finally, when they get home, they are tired and starving, so they eat whatever they can find to hold them over until dinner, their first real meal of the day.

And because they really have not eaten all day, they continue to snack all evening. This is a recipe for fatigue and obesity.

I know you think you are not a breakfast person, but you have been fasting all night! The word *breakfast* means you are *breaking* your *fast!* Eat something before you go to school, even if you must get up fifteen minutes earlier to do so. Then you will not need to keep a drawer full of candy in your desk to get you through the day.

Keep in mind that nutrition affects your reactions to stress. If you are hungry or lacking in vitamins, you will overreact to that student who constantly gets on your last nerve. Do you really want to have to apologize tomorrow for the cruel words you said in hunger today?

The adage says: Breakfast like a king, lunch like a working man, and supper like a pauper. This may be more than you can handle right now, but do not skimp on your meals.

Sleep well.

Everything I said about the need to eat well can also be applied to the need to sleep well. I know that during college you learned how to get along on almost no sleep, but the decisions you made in college affected only you. Now your decisions affect over a hundred other people, and it is your job to teach them well.

You already know what the experts say about getting enough sleep: get at least six to eight hours a night, turn off your electronics at least an hour before bedtime, keep your bedroom cool and dark. As a teacher, you should also stop grading or planning at least an hour before bedtime. Your brain will keep working while you sleep, and you really do not want it grading papers all night! I say this from experience; I have had plenty of nights when my dreams were all about the papers I graded right before bed. That is not a recipe for sleeping well.

Sometimes your brain will not shut off and let you sleep, or you will fall into an exhausted sleep just to wake up a few hours later worrying about how you will get everything done. (I used to wake up worrying about how my junior class would pay for the prom.) The best tip I can give you is to write it all down. Go ahead and get up; you are not sleeping anyway. Sit down with a pen and paper (or dictate into your phone) and write down everything that is in your head. Amazingly, once it is down on paper, your brain will feel relieved of its burden and let you sleep.

Substitute Teachers

In our district, substitute teachers can choose which teachers they will cover—and which teachers they will not cover. As you might imagine, that means that good substitutes can be choosy and are in high demand, so keeping them happy is a priority.

I have always told my students that I knew the substitutes long before I knew my students and that I would continue to have a relationship with my subs long after my students had left me; therefore, I would believe whatever the sub told me. Even if the whole class sided against the sub, I would believe the adult over the students. Their job as students was to behave in such a way that the sub would have no reason to tell me anything bad.

I also told students that whatever work they did for a substitute would count double. I reminded them that I never left busy work, and the work I left with a sub was just as important as what I assigned in class. Since I knew they often did not take sub work seriously, that work would impact their grade harder than regular class work.

Develop a relationship with your substitute teachers. You may not know your sub well, since he is there when you are absent, but most substitutes work the same schools all the time, so make the time to visit with them when they are in someone else's class.

Let me stress again the need to be organized. Leave lesson plans that are easy to follow. Use bullet comments rather than paragraphs (yes, you, English teacher!) because when they are in the middle of class, subs need to be able to find information easily, not look for it in the middle of a wordy paragraph. I even print my substitutes' lesson plans on colored paper to help them keep track of it during the day.

Leave your seating chart and attendance sheet under your lesson plan in the middle of your desk. Leave a couple of pens and pencils accessible on your desk as well.

Make all the copies your sub will need for the day and label them with sticky notes so your sub will know which period will use which copies. If you need your students to use a textbook, tell the sub in your lesson plans where those books are. Your students will lie to the sub. They will say that they do not have this book in class. They will say that you did this lesson yesterday. Be as specific as you can so that the sub can have confidence in your lesson.

When I left a movie for a sub, I always left questions for students to answer with the movie. Sometimes I also left the answer key for the sub, but I stapled it to the lesson plan so that it did not get handed out to students. In my lesson plan, I would ask the sub to write down where the movie left off so I could continue it the next day.

Tell the sub whether to collect work at the end of the period or to tell students to keep it until tomorrow. When I knew my subs well, I would leave them the choice: tell students it is due at the end of the period, but if you see that they are working hard and need more time, you may tell them to finish it for homework.

Not all substitute teachers are great. If you are lucky, you will have a retired teacher who really enjoys being in the classroom, but some are just there for the paycheck. When the latter happens, you may have to be flexible when you return to class and reteach some information; however, do your best not to say anything bad about the sub to your students. Always give the sub the benefit of the doubt. Otherwise you risk sending a message to your students that you will believe them over the adult in the room.

Open House/Parent Night

When you are new to teaching, meeting groups of parents can be scary. Even as we gain experience, many teachers who are comfortable talking to groups of students get nervous about talking to their parents. Here are some tips that I have found helpful:

1. Have a form for them to fill out. Most schools like to have a sign-in sheet so they can know how many parents attended, but I always hated having a line of parents waiting to sign in. My husband gave me the idea of having a half-page form instead. It asks parents the student's name, the parents' names, their preferred contact mode (phone call, text, email), and any other information they want me to know (she should wear

82

glasses but refuses to, he needs to sit near the board, they care for a sick grandmother at home and he might be absent a lot, *etc.*). Have these forms on a table near the door, along with a stack of pens or pencils (that you know will disappear), and file them in your student information binder when you are done. Then as parents come in, you can direct them to fill out the form while you are talking to other parents.

2. Keep a seating chart handy. Our open house always took place within the first couple weeks of school starting, giving me little time to learn students' names and faces. If parents asked me about their child, I could look quickly at the seating chart and see their assigned seat. Parents seemed to enjoy knowing where their child sat in my class, but it helped me to picture their child and speak more confidently about them.

3. Have copies of your syllabus available for parents. Be prepared to tell them what you will cover this year in class, how much homework parents should expect to see each week, what projects you have coming up, and what extra credit you have available. I also told parents what testing was coming up, whether state competency tests for underclassmen or SAT/ACT for upper classmen, and how they could help their students prepare.

4. Print and post your grades. Of course, this means using student numbers and not names, and your grades should be up to date.

5. Do not ever talk about other students to parents. Even if those parents know more about their kids' friends than you do, you are legally obligated to keep your mouth shut. You can get into more trouble by talking about other students to people who are not their parents than just about anything else.

6. Open house is not the time for one-on-one conferences about student achievement. Some parents will try to corner you about their child, but you should point out that you have other parents waiting for your time and ask them to schedule an official parent conference.

Homework Passes

My favorite reward to give students, and their favorite reward to receive from me, was the homework pass. I gave freshmen homework almost every night, in addition to graded class assignments, so giving homework passes now and then did not inflate their grades at all, but it sure did motivate them!

Create a cute form on colored paper. Over many years of using the homework pass, I worried sometimes that students might copy them fraudulently, but it never happened. The only security I provided was to keep them out of sight in my filing cabinet and to sign them right before I handed them to students.

Homework Pass

Good for 100% on any assignment

Student _____

Assignment _____Date _____

Signature _____Date_____

Decide ahead of time how much the homework pass will be worth. I made mine worth 100% on any assignment (not test, quiz, or major project), but you could choose to let it add 30 or 50 points to anything. Just put that on the form you create, along with a signature line.

These were so much fun! I used them during class review competitions constantly, but I also used them intermittently when the discussion bogged down. Sometimes kids just don't care about a piece of literature you have to read, but when a kid gave a good answer, I would run over to my filing cabinet and pull out a homework pass for that kid. You can imagine the engagement from the rest of the class when they saw that. I also told students they would earn a homework pass if their parents came to open house. Then at open house I would give the pass directly to the parent and not to the kid. Parents became strong allies when I told them to save that pass for when they wanted to give it, like when their kids washed the car or cleaned the kitchen.

IEP/ESE/ESOL/504 Paperwork

You probably had plenty of coursework in teaching students with special needs, but nobody tells you how to handle all the paperwork that comes with those students. Within the first few weeks of school you will get copies of all the IEPs and 504 plans for your students. Unfortunately, like the emergency medical notifications, all of these come at once, too quickly for you to process the information.

As soon as the paperwork came to me, I typed the names of all my special-needs students. Then I went through their pages and pages of paperwork to find the specific needs and accommodations I was supposed to meet and typed those under their names. Print this list and keep it handy, but not where other students can access it. I kept mine in my attendance folder at first, but eventually I kept it on my laptop, password protected. During the first month or two of school, I kept this list in front of me as I planned my lessons and made sure that my lesson plans included the necessary accommodations. After a while, I knew the students well enough not to need the list anymore.

In most states, you are expected to document that you gave the students their accommodations. An easy way to do this is to write the date under the students' names on your list. Then in your lesson plan write out what you did to accommodate the students' needs. Your school may have specific forms you have to fill out for accommodations, but this is a good place to start.

Religion, Politics, and Worldview

Teachers often fall too far to one side or the other: they talk too much about their worldview or they are afraid to mention it at all. For this discussion, we will use the word *worldview* to cover the whole category that also includes religious and political views.

On the one hand, I knew a teacher who was fired and lost his certification because, among other things, he terrorized the Christians in his class. He told them they were stupid for believing in God and treated them differently from other students. We all have a worldview, but we do not have the right to make students feel ashamed of theirs.

On the other hand, I too often hear teachers apologize for discussing literature that has any mention of religion in it, as though religion is a taboo subject that has no place in school. How can you teach western literature without a discussion of Christian themes?

87

How can you teach middle eastern literature without a discussion of Islam?

For the last five years of my career, I taught Advance Placement Language and Composition. One-half of the course and the final exam is argument, so my job was to teach students how to argue powerfully without alienating their audience. The best way for me to do that was to demonstrate it all year. I brought in current news articles and assigned students to write a response. Then I verbally critiqued their responses, focusing primarily on their logic and technique.

As I started teaching argument, I told my students my background and my religious beliefs and then reassured them that their beliefs would not affect their standing in my class. In fact, some students related a conversation to me later in the year. They asked a boy in my class whom they knew to have the same religious beliefs that I hold whether he got easier treatment from me. His answer, backed up by other students in that class, was that I held him to a higher standard since he represented what I believed as well. I did not let him get away with any poor logic while he was arguing my preferred side of the issue!

The point here is that we all have a worldview. You do not have the right to hurt or prefer your students based on their worldviews, but you do not need to keep yours a secret.

Standardized Testing

When I first started teaching, standardized testing was relatively rare. Students were tested once or twice in elementary years and then had to pass a state graduation exam in high school. Others also chose to take the SAT or ACT.

Now, all kids test, starting in third grade in most states. That means that regardless of what grade or subject you teach, you will probably have to proctor a standardized test.

Why did I dedicate a section to this? After all, you write tests and give them in your class all the time. The reason is that doing something wrong while you proctor a standardized test can cause you to lose your job or even your certification.

When you get the teacher's manual for the test you must proctor, read it! You do not need to read the whole thing, but you do need to read all the sections that apply to proctors, the people administering the test. Use sticky notes to tab it and highlight it. In one color, highlight everything you have to say—and say it verbatim! In another color, highlight everything you must do and when you must do it. The manual will tell you when to pass out which paper, and you should follow those instructions to the letter.

Everything I have said in this book so far has been encouraging to you (I hope), but this should add a little stress to you. Nothing about this test is worth losing your job, so do not take short cuts. Before you start the test, find out (in the manual) what you can say to students when they ask questions about the test. Are you allowed to read questions to them? Are you allowed to paraphrase the instructions? The testing manuals are specific, and if you cannot find the answer, you should ask the administrator who oversees testing.

If your own students are in your testing group, you may be very tempted to give hints or helps. DO NOT DO IT! Ask yourself again, "Is this worth losing my job?" You want your students to do well, but resist. Trust yourself and them. You have taught them well; let them show what they have learned on their own.

Chapter Seven

Encouragement

Teaching is one of the hardest jobs ever. Listen to the responses when you tell someone for the first time what you do for a living. "Oh, I could never do that!" followed by "(Your subject) was my favorite" or "I hated (your subject)". One week the press will call you a hero; the next week you will be enemy number one. The same people who declare that they could never do your job will deride you for having too many holidays and summers off.

In school, you will get tired of older teachers calling you a young pup. Every young teacher has a story about a custodian who mistook her for a student—hold onto that story because you will enjoy it when you get older. Do not let your youth be a problem for you.

You have energy that older teachers wish they still had. You need that energy to make up for your lack of experience, but your students will enjoy the life you bring to your classroom, and older teachers will feel rejuvenated when they are around you.

You have fresh ideas that older teachers will enjoy as well. I always learned as much from my interns as they learned from me. Because they were right out of college, they had new and creative ways to teach concepts that I had never considered before.

You know technology better than the teachers around you, so be their tech support. In exchange, they will enjoy sharing their experience with you. Be that teacher who tries all the new stuff. I will let you in on a secret: it is harder to change the way you have always done things than it is to learn it the first time. When our state considered moving from our long-time state standards to Common Core, I asked my principal to move me to a different grade. I knew that I would be too tempted to teach things the way I always had, but moving to a new grade would force me to integrate the new ways as I learned the new material.

If your school still uses the ESE co-teach model, volunteer to be a co-teacher. I learned as much from having another teacher in the classroom as I did in college, because now I saw how all that theory I had learned became reality in the classroom.

Teaching is as much art as it is science, but as with any other art, if you can get the science down pat, the art will come.